Sir Francis Drake

PETER LELY
and JAMES MILDREN

Introduction

Sir Francis Drake rose from humble origins to become one of the most famous Englishmen. His exploits brought him wealth and popularity. He epitomised the essence of Protestantism – the belief in democracy and the respect for the individual. His deep faith, nurtured from childhood by his father, drove him in search of the Catholic Spanish colonists in the New World. He accumulated a vast fortune derived from the spoils of his bold attacks on the Spanish ships and settlements, which was skilfully used to buy property and to finance further expeditions in support of Queen Elizabeth's conflicts with Philip II of Spain. The treasure that Drake seized on his voyage round the world paid for Elizabeth's government for a whole year, and his harassment of the Spanish Main demoralised Spain and weakened her empire.

Drake was a talented navigator and his journeys did much to expand the knowledge of the oceans. As a captain, he was respected by his men. Although he could be ruthless, he was courteous and honourable. He took opportunities as they presented themselves, and showed no fear in leading boarding parties or capturing towns and settlements. Later, at Cadiz and in the English Channel against the Armada, he showed all the skills of a brilliant commander.

Drake endured a lifetime of privations, living on board infected ships in unkind climates for months on end. On the rare occasions when he was on land, he returned to his birthplace, the West Country, buying property and supporting his countrymen as a Member of Parliament. He worked on defences for Plymouth and organised the town's water supply.

By his knighthood in 1581, Drake gained public recognition of his achievements, and the purchase of Buckland Abbey represented a material display of his importance. His coat-of-arms, carved over a fireplace at Buckland, contains the motto, *Sic parvis magna* – 'Thus great achievements from small beginnings'.

Portrait of Sir Francis Drake by Marcus Gheeraerts, the Younger

Childhood

Francis Drake was born on Lord Russell's Crowndale estate near Tavistock in Devon, probably in the year 1540. His father, Edmund Drake, is believed to have been a cottager or tenant on the estate. The family had few advantages in life, apart from being related to the influential Hawkyns family of Plymouth. At the time of Drake's birth, the great William Hawkyns was nearing the end of a dazzling career as sailor, adventurer and naval advisor to Henry VIII. He had two sons, John and William, both more than ten years older than Drake, who were to play an important part in Drake's future career.

When Henry VIII broke off relations with the Church of Rome, and made himself Supreme Head of the English Church, he saw his power diminished by the presence in England of Catholic monasteries and convents, which owned almost a third of the country. This concentration of wealth and influence was still under the control of the Pope in Rome. Henry made moves to dissolve the monasteries, and sold them to his noblemen. Protestantism slowly became the main religion in England.

Drake's father was a Protestant lay-preacher and was no doubt supported by the Russells. John Russell, first Earl of Bedford, had associated closely with Henry VIII in his policy of the dissolution of the Catholic monasteries. But the West Country was still one of the strongholds of the Old Faith and, when the new Prayer Book of Edward IV was ordered to be read in all churches at Whitsun 1549, there was a violent uprising against the reformers. 'In a week the west country was ablaze, all favourers of the new book were flying for their lives, the gentry were hiding in woods and caves, and Lord Russell, who was sent down to restore order, found that he could not move nearer to his home than Honiton.'

The Drakes, along with many other Protestants, fled, first to the comparative safety of the seaport of Plymouth and their kinsmen, the Hawkyns, and then on to the southern banks of the Thames Estuary at Gillingham in Kent, where they lived on an old naval hulk. It was from here that Drake's father continued his preaching and his wife raised the family. (They had twelve sons in all.) This strange creaking hulk, moving with the tides and set in mud and eddying currents was the home of Francis Drake from the age of about eight onwards. His childhood was spent rowing and sailing small boats through narrow tideways and estuaries, learning of the wind and fickle currents. The English fleet was anchored at the nearby royal shipyard at Chatham and his father, now a preacher in the fleet, would move from ship to ship.

The seamen of the east coast were stoutly Protestant, and so it was natural that, by the age of fourteen, Francis Drake had been taken as an apprentice on a small bark trading between the Medway and Holland and France. The bark was shallow and broad-beamed, with a single sail, and carried loads of grain, cloth and leather. It was during this time on the North Sea that Drake developed great skill in navigation, learning to pilot the boat through the hazards of tidal channels with hidden sand-banks. When the master of the bark died, he left his boat to Drake, an act which clearly shows the respect he felt for the young man.

The farmhouse at Crowndale in whose grounds stood Drake's home

Early adventures

Now in his early twenties, Drake was master of his own bark. He was a vain and elegant young man. His contemporary, the historian John Stow, describes him thus: '. . . low of stature, of strong limb, round headed, brown hair, full-bearded, his eyes round, large and clear, well-favoured face, and of a cheerful countenance'.

But Drake was restless. Spanish armies were becoming an increasing threat in France and the Low Countries. The main export trade of cloth to the busy port of Antwerp was affected. Restrictions on trade increased on both sides of the Channel and animosity grew. Protestants began making revenge attacks on Spanish ships in the English Channel. In 1564, Spain seized as many English vessels as she could find, and this effectively stopped all trade across the Channel. It was at this moment that Drake was given the opportunity to accompany Captain John Lovell on a trading expedition to Spain. He sold his bark and set sail with Lovell from Plymouth.

The following year, Drake sailed as second-in-command under Lovell to the African coast, where they were to pick up slaves needed in the rapidly expanding Spanish colonies in the Americas. The ships turned west from the African coast, loaded with human cargo, and headed for the fabled Indies on the Spanish Main. This was Drake's first experience of ocean sailing, of trade winds and of deep-sea navigation. At Rio de la Hacha, just east of Panama, Drake first encountered Spanish treachery. In later life he was curiously secretive about this incident, but it is thought that Lovell and Drake entered the port to sell slaves at the invitation of the Spanish merchants, only to witness the seizure of their cargo without payment.

Whatever happened at Rio de la Hacha, the incident served to further Drake's growing determination to fight and defeat the Spanish. They could not be trusted. They were dishonest in their trading methods and, more to the point, they were Catholics – antichrists. Like his father, Drake was an intensely religious man. The Spanish were becoming, in the eyes of Drake, oppressive and evil, and just four years later he was to witness Spanish betrayal and massacre at San Juan de Ulua which was to strengthen his resolve in his crusade against Spain and Catholicism.

Miniature of Sir Francis Drake by Nicholas Hilliard, a friend and fellow Devonian, painted after Drake's return from his voyage round the world

The Spanish Main

Since the discovery of the Indies by Columbus, in 1492, Spain and Portugal had been slowly claiming land, moving from the relatively poor islands of Cuba and Jamaica to the mainland of Mexico, Colombia and Peru. Here, vast reserves of gold, emeralds and silver were discovered. By the middle of the sixteenth century, the Spanish empire in the Americas was well established.

No foreigners were allowed to settle or trade in the Spanish colonies without a royal licence from Madrid. These were difficult to obtain. Both French and English seamen wished to trade

with the Spanish, but without the formal approval of the government this became increasingly difficult. French and English privateers thus carried documents from their own governments which allowed them to attack and capture Spanish ships. After all, what right did the Spanish have to the benefits of any lands outside the kingdom of Spain?

Out of this confusion emerged one man, Drake's cousin, John Hawkyns. His grand plan was to break the Spanish trading monopoly and to challenge the Spanish claim to be 'Lordes of halfe the world' by means of peaceful co-existence.

With the financial help of a London-based syndicate, he hoped to trade with the Spanish and Portuguese, offering,

The north-east trade winds and prevailing currents carried trading vessels from Spain and Portugal across the Atlantic to the islands of the West Indies and the Spanish Main. Ships returned through the Florida Channel and were taken homeward by westerly winds and the Gulf Stream

Key

Trade winds

Currents

ÆTATIS SVÆ LVIII
Anno Dni 1591

amongst other things, slaves from West Africa to work in the mines and on the plantations. He also offered to police the Caribbean against pirates. On his first two voyages he traded slaves with the colonists and successfully managed to intimidate the privateers on the north-west coast of South America – the Spanish Main.

Hawkyns' second enterprise was partly sponsored by Queen Elizabeth I, who lent him her ship, the *Jesus of Lübeck*. But rather than improving relations with Spain, Hawkyns' honest and worthy trading intentions made the Spanish king, Philip II, suspicious, for he feared the infiltration of Protestants into his colonies and the disastrous effect this would have on Spain's domination of much of the known world.

By 1567 the relationship between England and Spain was deteriorating. Hawkyns prepared for his third expedition, again supported by the Queen, who lent him the *Jesus of Lübeck* and the *Minion.* A secret plan was devised to disrupt Spanish colonial trade and capture the ships loaded with the treasure that Spain depended upon. Drake joined his kinsman Hawkyns as commander of the *Judith,* one of the ten ships in the fleet. But things went badly wrong from the start. The Spanish suspected Elizabeth's intentions and attempted to foil Hawkyns' plans to leave Plymouth. Then the fleet had to endure terrible storms in the Bay of Biscay. On the Guinea coast a number of losses were suffered as the men attempted to ambush Africans who, having grown accustomed to European ways, defended themselves with poisoned darts. Having captured only a small number of slaves, Hawkyns and Drake sailed west to the Indies and there, over a period of two months, traded manufactured goods.

Philip of Spain had sent word to the colonists not to trade with Hawkyns, but many settlers did and others were persuaded by force. When the fleet arrived at Rio de la Hacha, the scene of Drake's first encounter with the Spanish, Drake spared no time in acting in his own forceful manner for, '. . . we chased and drove the [Spanish boat] to the shore . . . We landed and planted

Portrait of Sir John Hawkyns by Hieronymus Custodis

on the shore . . . our field-ordinance: we drove the Spaniards up into the country above 2 leagues, whereby they were enforced to trade with our general, to whom he sold most part of his negroes.'

After moving on to Cartagena to replenish stores, and sell off the last remaining slaves, Hawkyns' ships headed for home. They sailed north-west and then east, attempting to pass through the Florida Channel and out into the Gulf Stream. In the Channel they ran into a storm and were forced back, with no alternative but to land on the Mexican coast at San Juan de Ulua (Veracruz). It was from this port that the annual treasure-ship from Mexico set sail for Spain.

By a curious coincidence, the vessel, with its accompanying fleet of thirteen ships, was due to arrive from Spain to collect the treasure, and the settlers, believing Hawkyns' ships to be their own, rowed out and greeted them enthusiastically. Only as they were boarding did they spot the royal standard of England flying from the leading ship. Panic broke out on the small boats and on shore. Hawkyns attempted to reassure them that he had come in peace. He would dearly have liked to have sailed immediately, but his fleet of ten ships badly needed provisions and repairs. The following morning the great treasure-ship arrived, carrying the new Viceroy of Mexico. He assumed that Hawkyns had seized the port, and tense negotiations went on for four days. Then, on 21 September, it was agreed that the English might repair their ships and take on stores. But Hawkyns remained wary and settled his fleet by a small off-shore island.

On the following night the truce was broken. The Spanish massacred the men on shore and sent ships in to sink the English fleet. Of the ten ships, eight were abandoned, including the Queen's ship, the *Jesus of Lübeck*. Only two, under Hawkyns and Drake, escaped. Early in 1569, after terrible privations, the *Judith* and the *Minion* finally arrived back in Plymouth. It was the end of Hawkyns' experiments in diplomacy. Drake never

A Portuguese carrack, used for trading and to carry treasure from the Indies to the port of Lisbon

forgot this experience and, as a result, waged a personal war against Spain for the rest of his life.

On 4 July 1569 Drake married Mary Newman, whose brother had sailed with him on the recent expedition. They were married at St Budeaux near Plymouth. We have no portrait of her and there were no children. Mary was to see very little of her husband and died thirteen years later.

Drake's first view of the Pacific

Drake was now about thirty and, with the financial help of the Hawkyns brothers, he set sail once more for the West Indies. For the next three years he made carefully planned reconnaissance expeditions to assess the colonies on the Spanish Main. In 1572-3, with his two small ships, the *Swan* and the *Pascha,* Drake headed for the coast of Panama. He had discovered that the treasures of Peru were shipped up the west coast of South America to the Isthmus of Panama, where they were transferred to pack mules and taken across to Nombre de Dios on the Caribbean. Vast quantities of gold and silver were then stored on the coast, ready to be transported back to Spain.

Drake attacked Nombre de Dios and, although he succeeded in reaching the treasure-house, only a small amount of the treasure was taken. In the skirmish he was wounded in the leg, and his crew, fearing for his life, carried him back to the ships. He had lost so much blood '. . . that it soon filled the very prints that our footsteps made, to the great dismay of all our company, who thought it not credible that one should be able to lose so much blood and live'.

Drake recovered his strength and began to plan a raid on the pack route, but it was still three months before the end of the rainy season and there was time to harass Spanish settlements. This, he hoped, would draw the authorities' attention away from his plans for a mainland raid.

In January, news came that the mule-trains, laden with gold and silver from the mines of Peru, were making their way through the dense forest to Nombre de Dios, where the Spanish treasure-fleet was waiting. Drake and his raiding party set off, guided by a group of Cimaroons who knew the terrain intimately. These descendants of escaped negro slaves, who inhabited the thick jungle, hated their former masters, the Spanish. Their leader told Drake of a high point in the mountains where both the Atlantic and the Pacific could be seen. On 11 February 1573 Drake reached this point and, climbing a tree to a lookout platform, he sighted the Pacific for the first time.

The contemporary historian, William Camden wrote, 'He was so vehemently transported with desire to navigate that sea, that falling down there upon his knees, he implored the Divine assistance that he might, at some time or other, sail thither and make a perfect discovery of the same; and thereunto he bound himself with a vow. From that time forward, his mind was pricked on continually night and day to perform this vow.'

It was time to head down to the plains around Nombre de Dios, where Drake ambushed the treasure-trains and, after many adventures, succeeded in reboarding his ships at the mouth of the Rio Francisco. Earlier he had had to abandon the *Pascha* and the *Swan* because of their poor condition, but he had managed to capture two Spanish vessels, one filled with provisions. On 9 August 1573 Drake and his men arrived back in Plymouth with their treasure, leaving the Spanish Main in a state of agitation.

The Spanish settlers were to write to Philip II: 'We entreat Your Majesty to remedy the grievous conditions prevailing today in the Indies. For every two ships that come hither from Spain, twenty corsairs appear . . . They go so far as to say they are Lords of the Sea and the Land – Unless Your Majesty deign to favour all this coast by remedying the situation, all these settlements must necessarily be abandoned.'

Drake was now a very rich man and, from his gains, purchased lands and property in Plymouth. News of his exploits spread among his fellow countrymen and he became a popular hero. Although she was pleased, Queen Elizabeth was not able to acknowledge Drake's success. Her relationship with Philip II was calmer and it was not the moment to admit the presence of two captured Spanish ships, just arrived from the Indies, loaded with treasure.

Wisely, Drake slipped away to Ireland. Little is known about how the next two years were spent, but it is believed he served with Walter Devereux, Earl of Essex, who was endeavouring to pacify Antrim. It was in Ireland, however, that Drake met and grew to know Thomas Doughty, a gentleman and scholar employed as a lawyer by the Earl of Essex.

The harbour of Nombre de Dios

Expedition to the Pacific

By 1576, relations with Spain had deteriorated again and Drake was back in England. Thomas Doughty had also returned and was employed as secretary to Christopher Hatton, Captain of the Guard, and a new favourite of Queen Elizabeth. It was through his friendship with Doughty that Drake achieved an introduction to Francis Walsingham, Secretary of State, who was a close ally of Robert Dudley, the powerful Earl of Leicester.

There was at this time much talk of exploration. In 1574 Sir Richard Grenville, supported by a West Country syndicate of investors, had planned an expedition around the coast of South America, through the Straits of Magellan and into the Pacific Ocean in search of *terra australis,* a vast unknown continent which was believed to exist in the southern hemisphere, balancing the land masses of the north. Grenville had hoped to return home by way of a north-west passage which was thought to link the Pacific with the Atlantic. However, the idea had to be abandoned when the government refused to grant permission for the venture, because the expedition would inevitably pass through waters controlled by the Spanish on its voyage north through the Pacific, and might endanger the fragile peace existing at the time.

The government, led by William Cecil, Lord Burghley, Elizabeth's Lord Treasurer and chief minister, showed more interest in finding a north-west passage to the Pacific by allowing Martin Frobisher to sail for North America in 1576. If a way could be found to reach the Pacific in the northern hemisphere, trade with lands bordering this ocean would be made much easier. Frobisher discovered a strait which he claimed was the entry to the north-west passage, and in subsequent expeditions found Hudson's Strait and Hudson's Bay.

In 1577 a syndicate was formed in London which included the recently knighted Sir Christopher Hatton, the Earl of Leicester, Francis Walsingham, Lord Admiral Lincoln, Sir William Winter

Portrait of Sir Richard Grenville, Drake's rival

AN° · DNI · 1571
ÆTATIS · SVÆ
· 29 ·

(Surveyor of the Navy), his brother, George Winter (Clerk of the Queen's ships) and John Hawkyns, who was soon to be Treasurer of the Navy. The aim of this group was to finance and equip an expedition to pass through the Magellan Straits and into the Pacific Ocean in order to seek out new lands not dominated by Spain, lying to the south of the Magellan Straits. Trading agreements would be signed with the inhabitants of *terra australis incognita.* Although Grenville was considered for the command of this expedition, Francis Drake was chosen.

Drake was summoned by Francis Walsingham to meet the Queen, who had a secret involvement in the plan. Walsingham hinted that Elizabeth would be interested in taking revenge on Philip of Spain through this venture, a view which was confirmed by the Queen's own words to Drake. An agreement was reached that, on passing through the Straits of Magellan, Drake would sail north to raid the treasure-ships of Spain in the Pacific, where attack was least expected. The Queen insisted that Burghley, who remained strongly in favour of making peace with Spain, should not know anything of the plan.

On 15 November 1577 Drake sailed out of Plymouth on his flagship, the *Pelican,* a ship of about 100 tons carrying an armament of eighteen guns, with the *Elizabeth,* of 80 tons and with sixteen guns and commanded by John Winter (the son of George Winter), the *Marigold,* of 30 tons, also well armed, the *Swan,* a newly built storeship of 50 tons, and the *Benedict,* of 15 tons, captained by Thomas Moone, a skilled carpenter who had gone with Drake on earlier voyages. The ships carried the parts for four small pinnaces, which could be quickly assembled and used to explore inshore waters.

Drake took care to see that the *Pelican,* which had a double-sheathed hull, was in especially good condition and took with him 'rich furniture', including silver plates and cutlery, perhaps partly to impress the local inhabitants of countries that they might visit. There were fiddlers to provide music, and drums for music-making and signalling.

Portrait of Lord Burghley, for forty years the Queen's chief advisor

The sailors and the general public in Plymouth were told that the ships would sail to Alexandria, where a trading agreement would be reached with the Ottoman empire. The officers and gentlemen-adventurers were told the official plan – to make contact with *terra australis*. It seems likely, however, that, despite all the precautions, Lord Burghley at least already knew the real aim of the journey and that he had been told by Drake's close friend, Thomas Doughty, who, with his younger brother, John, was aboard the *Pelican*.

The small fleet made its way along the Cornish coast, but ran into a gale so fierce that the *Pelican* was damaged and the expedition was forced to return to Plymouth for repairs.

The ships finally set sail on 13 December, carrying a total of 164 men and boys, including the Doughty brothers, Francis Fletcher, the chaplain, Drake's youngest brother, Thomas, and his nephew, John Drake, who at fourteen was employed as Drake's page.

The seamen did not realise their true destination until the coast of Morocco was reached. The Magellan Straits were notoriously difficult to navigate – even the Spaniards preferred not to use them. From this time on, the crews' natural anxieties about the dangers of the voyage were secretly played upon by Thomas Doughty, who, unknown to Drake, was probably following Burghley's wishes to hamper the expedition in order to avoid conflict with Spain.

Off the coast of Morocco, Drake took control of a Portuguese ship of 40 tons, offering the crew the 15-ton *Benedict* in exchange. The new craft was named the *Christopher*, in honour of Sir Christopher Hatton. The fleet then sailed further south to the Cape Verde Islands in order to take on fresh water and provisions. Another Portuguese ship, the *Maria*, was captured, yielding more food and 'a good store of wine'. Bound for Brazil, the ship also carried a Genoese pilot, Nuño da Silva, who was familiar with the Brazilian coastline. Thomas Doughty was given charge of the rechristened *Mary*, with its Portuguese crew. Drake's younger brother, Thomas, was also put on board, with the trumpeter, Tom Brewer.

The fleet continued amongst the islands to La Brava, the last port of call before crossing the Atlantic, where Drake put ashore the captured Portuguese crew. The pilot, da Silva, was compelled to continue with the expedition. It was at La Brava that the first real hint of trouble came. Drake's trumpeter, Brewer, accused Doughty of taking some of the Portuguese cargo. Doughty denied this and suggested that the culprit was Drake's brother. Drake was furious and removed command of the *Mary* to his brother. Doughty was now to travel on the *Pelican*.

The voyage across the Atlantic was slow. Tensions grew among the seamen. The ships were becalmed for three weeks in the doldrums, and encountered sudden fogs, extreme heat and thunderstorms. It was 54 days before the company landed on the Brazilian coast in latitude 33 degrees south. Moving down the coast, the ships were scattered in the changeable weather, and eventually sought shelter in the mouth of the River Plate. Here, they stocked up with seal-meat and water, and then headed south towards Port St Julian, a large natural harbour used by Ferdinand Magellan sixty years earlier, during his voyage around the world.

At Port St Julian, the party was attacked by a group of Patagonians. Two men died. In their exploration of the area around the harbour, the crew found the gibbet on which the mutineers upon Magellan's ship had been hanged. During the crossing of the Atlantic, Doughty had encouraged the men's uneasiness and superstitions and had made much of their misfortunes. Perhaps he now felt it was his last chance to turn the expedition back. In Port St Julian, Drake finally lost patience with his former friend and ordered that Doughty should be brought to trial. He was accused of trying to overthrow the voyage and of witchcraft.

During the questioning it is likely that Doughty admitted having told Burghley the true purpose of the expedition. He was also accused of saying that the Queen and Council could be corrupted with money. The trial followed procedure usual in England at that time, and a jury of forty men finally agreed that

Doughty was a traitor and should be sentenced to death. Doughty and Drake took communion and ate a final meal together, drinking toasts, one to the other, before the execution took place, on 20 June 1578.

It was midwinter and the ships remained at Port St Julian for six weeks, waiting for the days to lengthen. Repairs were made, supplies gathered and morale was restored. Drake ordered each member of the crew to make a confession to chaplain Fletcher

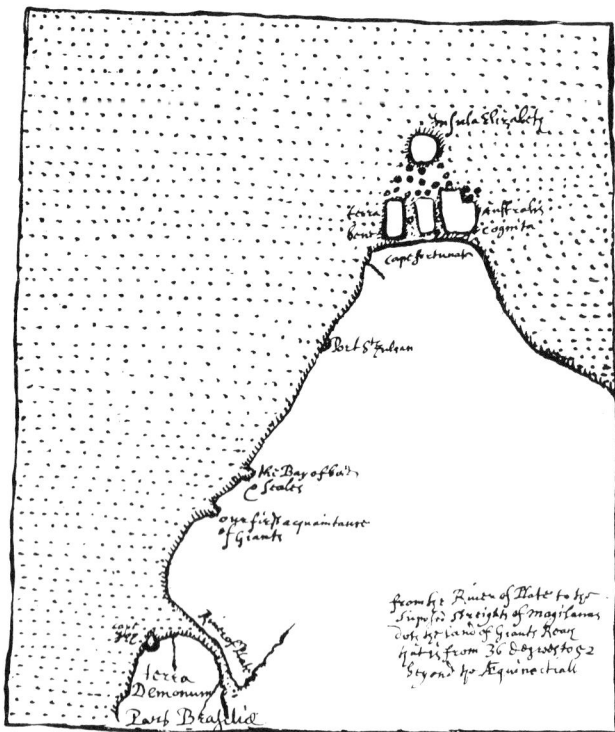

Map of South America from the River Plate, showing Port St Julian and the Magellan Straits

and to receive the sacrament. He then preached a sermon exhorting all men to give up quarrelling and to play their full part in the undertaking. A ship was available for any who wished to return to England. None took up the offer. Drake's determination and qualities of leadership were decisive at this stage in the expedition.

The *Swan* and the *Christopher* were broken up and the crews and stores taken aboard the three remaining ships. On 17 August 1578 the fleet weighed anchor, and within three weeks it had reached the opening of the Straits of Magellan. In the spirit of a new beginning, Drake renamed his flagship the *Golden Hind,* after the crest of Sir Christopher Hatton, Doughty's patron.

The Straits of Magellan and beyond

The weather was favourable and by great skill, using pinnaces to find a safe channel between the submerged rocks, the ships made their way through these hazardous waters in only sixteen days. Drake and his men became the first Englishmen to navigate the Straits of Magellan.

They had reached the Pacific, only to meet a fearsome gale which forced the fleet to drift helplessly southward. After a month the *Marigold* lost contact with the *Golden Hind,* never to be seen again. The *Golden Hind* and the *Elizabeth* were driven far south of the Straits and Drake realised that the Magellan Straits were not the only passage between the Atlantic and Pacific Oceans as had been believed. Tierra del Fuego was not the tip of a vast unknown continent, but merely an island.

The weather eventually eased, and the two ships made their way northwards to the coast of Chile, where, in a sudden squall, they finally parted company. The *Golden Hind* was driven southwards again, and Captain Winter, managing to regain the entry to the Straits, made the decision to turn the *Elizabeth* for home, arriving back safely with stories of Drake's exploits.

Sailing northward again, Drake searched in vain for the

A model of the Golden Hind, *the ship in which Drake sailed round the world*

Marigold and the *Elizabeth,* at last regaining the coast of Chile. In a small bay, contact was made with a friendly Indian fisherman who had news of a Spanish merchantman in the harbour at Valparaiso. Drake and his crew were able to take the Spanish sailors by surprise, and gained a good supply of wine and sufficient Bolivian gold to pay for the whole enterprise. Ashore, they raided the church, taking silver chalices, silks and altar cloths for the chaplain. They also made use of the opportunity to load up with fresh fruit and other supplies, the inhabitants of Valparaiso having made their escape to the hills. The master of the Spanish ship was captured for use as a pilot.

The *Golden Hind* set sail once more, heading north for Lima in Peru, the port where the Spanish treasure-ships took on their cargo. At Coquimbo, one man of a shore party in a pinnace was killed by Spaniards. However, a good anchorage was found a little further north and the crew set to work overhauling and repairing the ship. All preparations were made for the forthcoming attack on Lima.

Continuing northwards along the Chilean coast, Drake and his crew made the most of any opportunities that presented themselves. Members of a group collecting fresh water, who found a sleeping Spaniard with a bag of silver ingots beside him, reported, 'we took the silver and left the man'.

Finally reaching the harbour of Lima, Drake discovered twelve defenceless ships and took their cargo without difficulty. He then set sail to follow a rich treasure-ship which he was told was heading for Panama. *Nuestra Señora de la Concepcion,* otherwise known as the *Cacafuego,* was armed, but her captain suspected no danger, slowing his vessel to allow Drake to catch up with her. Drake attacked and captured the *Cacafuego* with his third shot, which broke her mizzenmast. His men swarmed aboard, returning with stores of a treasure beyond any expectations. It took several days to transfer the boxes of gold, silver, jewels and pearls to the *Golden Hind.* The captain of the Spanish vessel was treated with great courtesy, and was eventually put ashore unharmed, with messages for Captain Winter if they should ever meet.

The whole of the west coast of South America had by now had news of Drake's exploits and was alert to prevent further attacks, but Drake was still able to take the town of Guatulco, in Guatemala, in April. Prisoners were kept on the ship for three days while fresh supplies were taken on board, and were then released, together with Nuño da Silva, the pilot, who was to travel home via Panama.

The route home

Having captured as much treasure as the *Golden Hind* could carry, Drake had three possible routes back to England. The first was to return south, along a coastline alerted to his presence, to the Straits of Magellan, by now probably blockaded (or to the passage unknown to the Spanish to the south of Tierra del Fuego, with all the problems of unpredictable gales). The second was by attempting to find the north-west passage which was believed to exist between the Pacific and the Atlantic somewhere north of 40 degrees latitude. The third possibility was to return to England by sailing westward across the Pacific.

It seems likely that his first intention was to find the mythical north-west passage, since the *Golden Hind* continued to run northward well beyond latitude 40 degrees north, until the increasing cold and foggy weather led to the decision to turn south again. Landfall was made at latitude 38 degrees north in a bay on what is now the coast of California. The white cliffs on this part of the coast reminded Drake of Dover, and so he took possession of this land in the name of the Queen and called the place 'Nova Albion'.

The company stayed for five weeks, building a stockade, exploring inland and repairing the leaking *Golden Hind,* as they prepared for the long journey home. The local Indians were friendly, but rather in awe of the strangers who they thought might be gods, and they crowned Drake their king with a crown of feathers. Before leaving, Drake '. . . set up a monument of our being there, as also of Her Majesty's right and title to the same, namely a plate, nailed upon a fair great post'.

On 23 July the *Golden Hind* left Nova Albion, heading west across the Pacific. Land was not sighted again until the end of September, when she reached the Pulau Islands. The people here were hostile and stole Drake's goods, so he continued for a fortnight more and finally anchored at Ternate in the Moluccas or Spice Islands, where he found a friendly welcome.

The Sultan, who was at war with the Portuguese, seemed happy to make a trading agreement with the English. In later years, the friendly relationship between England and the Sultan and his son was to prove useful to the East India Company. The *Golden Hind* took on a cargo of cloves to add to the treasure already aboard, and sailed for the Celebes, where the ship was repaired, and the crew rested and recovered their strength.

For three weeks Drake and his crew tried to find their way through the islands in bad weather. Then disaster struck. On 9 January 1580, the *Golden Hind* ran aground on a hidden reef. In vain, the crew tried to heave her off. Part of the cargo of cloves was thrown overboard, together with eight of the big guns and various other items. The crew prayed. Suddenly the wind changed and the *Golden Hind* lifted herself off the reef and slipped into deep water. Because the hull of the ship was double-sheathed, no serious damage had been done.

The probable location of Nova Albion

It took another month before they were safely clear of the reefs and shoals and could head for Java, where they were welcomed and entertained by the local rajahs. Then news came of European ships in the area, and Drake decided it was time to leave. The *Golden Hind* set out to cross the Indian Ocean, rounding the Cape of Good Hope and sailing on until landfall was made on 22 July in Sierra Leone. Drake took aboard fresh

Drake's meeting with the Sultan of Ternate

Overleaf: *The 'Broadside Map' by Judocus Hondius of Amsterdam c. 1595, which shows the route of Drake's circumnavigation of the globe with (inset) details of his landings*

water and supplies and set off again two days later, not reaching Plymouth until 27 September 1580, almost three years after the voyage began.

Francis Drake had become the first Englishman to sail round the world. His first words to a local fisherman were, 'Is the Queen alive?' On being assured that she was, he sent a message to London informing Queen Elizabeth of his return.

Portus Nove Albionis

VERA TOTIVS EX

Descriptio D. Franc. Draci qui 5. navibus probè instructis, ex Anglia solvens 13
izferis partim flammis, partim fluctibus correptis, in Angliam rediit 27 Septem
Angli, qui eundem Draci cursū ferè tenuit etiam ex Anglia per universum
quinto Septembris 1588. in patriæ portum Plinmouth, unde prius ex

MONGOL
CIRCVLVS ARCTICVS
ANIAN
AMERI:

ASIA

Cathajo

INDIA ORIENTALIS

NOVA ALBION

TROPICVS CANCRI

MARE PACIFICVM

AEQVINOCTIALIS

NOVA GUINEA

MAR DI INDIA

TROPICVS CAPRICORNI

TERRA AVSTRALIS

CIRCVLVS ANTARCTICVS

GILOLO In.

um orbis ambitum circumnavigans, unica tantum navi, ingenti cum gloria
ITA est etiam viva delineatio navigationis Thomæ Candisth nobilis
temporis spacio: vigesimo primo enim Iulij 1586 navem conscendit, & decimo
um omnium admiratione reversus est. Iudocus Hondius.

Portus Iavæ Maioris

In hoc sinu Maioris portu Iosuam, qui tum epulta intervallo
interiectisibus eliquia partim in Insulam seu latet videt

CA

Nova
FLORI
DA
CO...PI.

MEXICANA

MARE

DEL
NORT
CARIBANA PARIA

H.B.Amazones

PE
RV

BRASILIA

Ch.S.Agustin
C.frio
Co.Blanco

RVSIA

Mare de Islandia
Baia

EVROPA

 ...AFRICA

MEDITERRANEVM

BARBARIA

BENIN

RABIA
DESERTA
ARABIA
FELIX

AFRI

CA

OCEANVS

ÆTHIOPICVS

OCEANVS

In his tabula miedine forti eligis, ut eodem
quæ facinis eliquid scimus uno sit confestis nobis
visuela sic pervenimus In Dovis Lõ Bant Gratul
eliquem, indebitur peperiant artmius hoc habit
hoc, vel gloriki etiam animariji literani nomina sit
val gloribis, ficto, navegavimus sando eliquid
sivimus Gracia Sibis sisscar colca & in sibi
ut Infinsura uscerpervenim nevegarimus sivimus

Navigation

The Elizabethans used a magnetic sea compass to determine their position. (Lodestones were carried on long journeys to remagnetise compass needles.) Speed was estimated by sand-glass, which measured half-hour intervals. It was not possible to calculate longitude at this time, but latitude could be ascertained to within ten or fifteen miles from the positions of the sun and stars, using an astrolabe, a quadrant or a cross-staff. A pair of compasses enabled the navigator to mark the ship's position on a chart. Perhaps the most important instrument, however, was the lead and line for sounding depth.

The development by the brilliant Elizabethan mathematician and astrologer, John Dee, of mathematical navigation methods gave a great advantage to English navigators.

Francis Drake was the outstanding English geographer and navigator of his time. He had learned the rudiments in the North Sea, and extended his knowledge through the accumulated

An astrolabe, used for finding latitude.
Opposite: *Drake's dial*

information gained by the Hawkyns family, who were excellent practical men. Clearly, however, he had at some stage studied geometry and astrology. For his voyage in 1570 to the West Indies, Drake had a 'dial' made which included a compass, tables of latitude and tides, and a quadrant.

Drake made full use of any information he could find. The pilot, Nuño da Silva noted that Drake possessed three books on navigation, one of these being Magellan's *Discovery,* a book describing his circumnavigation of the world. Da Silva noticed how Drake immediately sought out charts and navigational instruments from captured vessels, discarding those he did not require. He also had his own 'cards', or charts, one of which, nearly two yards wide, had been made for him in Lisbon by an expert cartographer.

On his voyage round the world Drake made important use of the pilots encountered aboard ships he captured. Between them, these men had good knowledge of the Brazilian, Chilean and Peruvian coasts, and of the route across the Pacific to the

Philippines, and they were familiar with the local weather patterns.

Drake was also concerned with adding to existing knowledge by sketching coastlines, and spent hours with his young nephew, John, painting and drawing harbours and coasts with serious practical intent.

Engraving of Sir Francis Drake by Hondius

Knighthood

The coat-of-arms granted to Drake in 1581. The ship at the top is being guided around the globe by the hand of God, and the shield symbolises the sea, with the two hemispheres

Drake's achievement was a brilliant demonstration of England's new power on the oceans. It raised her confidence and added to her prestige in Europe. Drake was summoned to London by Queen Elizabeth, and took with him gifts of emeralds, diamonds, gold and silver. His audience with the Queen lasted six hours. She ordered the *Golden Hind* to be brought round the coast from Plymouth to London. Drake dressed his ship with great banners of silk damask painted with gold, and on 4 April 1581 Elizabeth went in state to see the *Golden Hind* at Deptford and to partake in a sumptuous banquet. On the quarter-deck, in the presence of an excited crowd, the Queen knighted Drake. Elizabeth ordered that the *Golden Hind* was to be preserved, and the little ship lay in dry-dock at Deptford until she rotted away many years later.

Drake was now entitled to a coat-of-arms, and was seen to be in the Queen's favour. Elizabeth secretly allowed him to take £10,000 of the haul for himself and as much again for his crew, before any official accounting was done.

Buckland Abbey

Drake returned to Plymouth a famous and wealthy man. He became Member of Parliament for Bossinney, Cornwall, and in 1581–2 was Mayor of Plymouth. He began to look around for a country seat and this he found at Buckland Abbey, a few miles inland from Plymouth.

The abbey had been founded by the Cistercians in 1278, but since its dissolution, in 1539, had been the property of the Grenville family. It was presently owned by Sir Richard Grenville, the naval commander and privateer. He had spent a considerable amount of money to convert the abbey into a residence. Finding himself short of funds, he mortgaged the property in 1580 for £3,400 to Drake through his agents, John Hele and Christopher Harris, on the understanding that Drake would live there. Grenville did not repay the money, and in November 1582 Buckland Abbey became the property of Drake. Although Grenville and Drake were old rivals, they both saw advantages in transferring the ownership of Buckland. Drake was obviously happy with his new home, and Grenville probably knew how to dispose of Drake's secret hoards of gold and silver.

Drake was enjoying immense popularity and spending much time in London planning expeditions against the Spanish colonies. He purchased forty freehold properties in Plymouth from his kinsman, William Hawkyns, together with leasehold interests in Plymouth Town Mills, and became the third largest landowner in the town after the Hawkyns family and the Corporation.

Less than three months after Drake acquired Buckland, his first wife, Mary, died, having enjoyed only the briefest tenure as Lady Drake. In 1585 he married Elizabeth Sydenham, believed to have been a maid-of-honour to the Queen, and daughter and heiress of a rich landowner, Sir George Sydenham. They, too, had no children.

Right: *Portrait of Elizabeth Sydenham, Drake's second wife, by George Gower*

Buckland Abbey, Drake's Devon home for the last fifteen years of his life

Return to the Spanish Main

In these years Drake had seen no action at sea. He had been helping and advising John Hawkyns, Treasurer to the Navy. Hawkyns was supervising the building of a new fleet and improving conditions on board the ships.

Relations with Spain were growing more tense. Bernadino de

THE Famous West Indian voyadge made by the Englishe flete of 23. shippes and Barkes wher in ware gotten the Townes of S.IAGO : S.DOMINGO, CARTAGENA and S.AVGVSTINES the same beinge begon from Plimmouth in the Monneth of September 1585 and ended at Portesmouth in Iulie 1586 the whole conduct of the frude Voiadge beinge plainlie described by the pricked Line Newlie come forth by

Mendoza, the Spanish ambassador, wrote home to his king: 'They are building ships endlessly, and are thus making themselves masters of the sea. Seeing their country with such multitudes of ships helps to swell their pride, and they think that there is no prince on earth who can come against them.'

In September 1585 a fleet of twenty-three ships, two contributed by the Queen, set sail to the Spanish Main, with the aim of demoralising and crushing Spain's American empire once and for all. The total force of over 2,000 men was under the command of Sir Francis Drake. Over the next few months they raided and plundered the Spanish settlements mercilessly. Drake's main target, San Domingo, the capital of Cuba, was stormed and taken with little resistance. They attacked Cartagena, then sailed up the coast of Florida.

Before turning for home, Drake rescued 103 distressed English settlers from the new colony at Roanoke, Virginia. He reached England at the end of July 1586.

Although the expedition was not a financial success, it weakened the Spanish empire, demoralised the settlers and disrupted the economy. Payment to the Spanish armies in Europe was suspended.

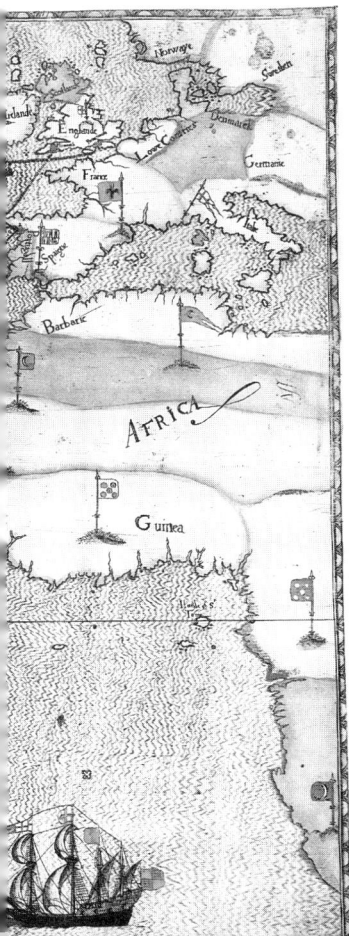

Map showing Drake's route to the Indies in 1585

'Singeing the King of Spain's beard'

For the whole of that year and into the spring of 1587, political tensions with Spain increased. In February, the Catholic Queen of Scotland, Mary Stuart, was executed. As claimant to the throne of England, she had been a constant threat to Elizabeth. With her death, the last hopes of Catholic succession appeared to have faded. However, Philip of Spain now laid claim to the throne through his marriage in 1554 to Henry VIII's eldest daughter, Mary I of England, who had died in 1558.

Philip had been preparing an attack on England for many months and the death of Mary Stuart prompted a fresh effort. He asked for invasion plans from his naval commander, the Marquis of Santa Cruz, and the chief of his armies in the Netherlands, Alexander Farnese, Duke of Parma.

Santa Cruz suggested a combined military and naval oper- ation, sailing from Spain with an armada of some 150 ships, 30,000 sailors, and 64,000 soldiers. Parma suggested an invasion in a single night from the Low Countries of 30,000 men, but requested a reinforcement of a further 30,000 to hold the Netherlands whilst the army was in England.

In the end, Philip decided that he would send the largest possible fleet to carry soldiers from Spain to meet Parma and his armies on the Netherlands' coast. Through a system of messengers, Parma would be kept informed of the progress of the fleet and prepare his forces to be ferried across the Channel to England on a convoy of barges.

News soon reached England from Spain of the preparations for Philip's great 'Enterprise of England' and the Queen instructed Drake to sail to the Spanish mainland and '. . . distress the ships within the havens themselves'. His fleet of twenty-three ships and 2,000 men set sail on 2 April 1587. *En route* he learned that a huge fleet was gathered at Cadiz. By 19 April he was outside the port and, without hesitation, sailed straight into the outer harbour, taking the Spanish by surprise. He succeeded in destroying or disabling most of the sixty ships moored there. As night fell, instead of retreating out to sea, Drake dropped

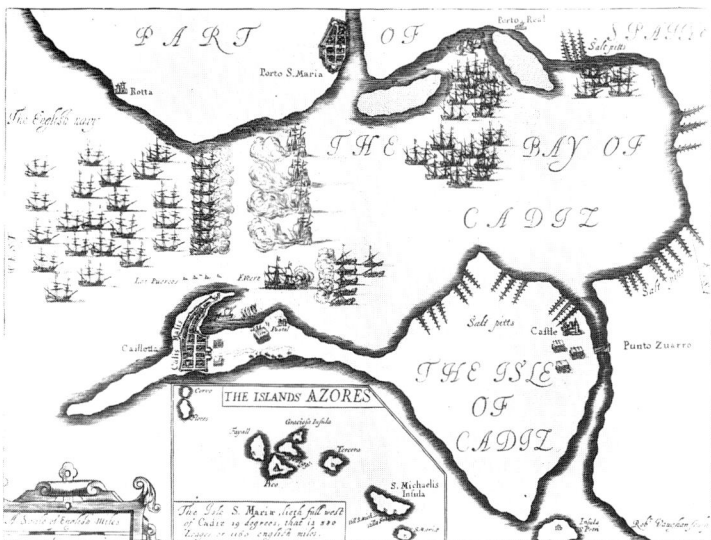

Map showing Drake's fleet attacking the harbour of Cadiz

anchor. The following morning he was surprised to see, hidden amongst the damaged ships, the enormous vessel belonging to Santa Cruz, the commander of the whole operation against England. This he captured and gutted, using only a fleet of small boats, then, after an agonising lull of wind, his ships were blown out of the harbour to safety.

Drake had been over thirty-six hours in Cadiz harbour, had destroyed some thirty ships and had seized six vessels laden with provisions. He then patrolled the Spanish coast for two months, crippling or sinking over 100 Spanish trading and fishing vessels. Amongst the items destroyed were casks and the seasoned oak to make them. Drake knew well that a fleet depended upon these for drinking water and provisions. This proved to be one of his most decisive actions. He later jokingly referred to the Cadiz episode as 'singeing the King of Spain's beard'. This extraordinarily brave action effectively delayed Spain's plans for an invasion of England for an entire year.

Preparations for the Armada

Slowly Spain resumed preparations for the Armada. In February 1588 the naval commander, Santa Cruz, died of age and exhaustion, and Philip appointed a landsman, the Duke of Medina Sidonia, aged 38, to take his place. The duke had little experience of warfare, and on hearing of the decision, he wrote to the king's secretary trying to excuse himself from the appointment, 'My health is not equal to such a voyage, for I know by experience of the little I have been at sea that I am always seasick and always catch cold. . . . Since I have had no experience of the sea, or of war, I cannot feel that I ought to command so important an enterprise.' Philip replied, 'All of what you say, I attribute to your excess of modesty. But it is I who must judge of your capabilities and parts, and I am fully satisfied with them.' Philip's judgement proved to be correct, for throughout the coming campaign Medina Sidonia was to show considerable courage and to prove a tenacious and efficient organiser of men and ships.

In England preparations were under way on land and sea to counter the Spanish threat. Charles, Lord Howard of Effingham was appointed Commander-in-Chief of the western fleet. Drake was his Vice-Admiral, with thirty-eight ships under his personal command. Three separate fleets were placed around the south coast, one at Dover, under Lord Henry Seymour, and the other two at Plymouth.

In early summer, Howard and Drake were ordered by the Queen to sail to Spain in a final attempt to halt the departure of the Armada. They set off from Plymouth and headed towards the northern Spanish town of Corunna, where Medina Sidonia was preparing his fleet for its imminent departure for England. In the Bay of Biscay, a change of wind forced them to return to Plymouth. It was this very wind that allowed Medina Sidonia to set sail for England, and his great Armada was sighted off the Lizard on 19 July 1588.

Portrait of Philip II of Spain

The battle begins

The Spanish fleet of 130 ships, 19,000 troops and 8,000 sailors was in a poor condition. The boats had seen long service and were leaking, and the crews were dying in large numbers from an epidemic. The casks containing food and water had been made from immature oak as a result of the shortage of seasoned wood caused by Drake's actions in the previous year. They leaked, or the contents turned bad. There was not enough money to pay the seamen and many had deserted, thus weakening the sailing ability of the fleet. The design of the boats had changed little over the years. They still retained high defensive castles fore and aft. They were large and strongly built and ideally suited for Atlantic passages. Sailing west, they would catch the north-east trade winds, returning on the Atlantic westerlies. The English ships, as the Spanish were to find to their cost, were lower, faster (by one knot) and could lie closer to the wind. The design of the English vessels had evolved through the need to manoeuvre into difficult harbours in the English Channel.

When news came in the afternoon of 19 July 1588 of the approaching fleet, Howard and Drake are said to have been playing bowls (possibly a form of French *boules* on gravel) on Plymouth Hoe. Tradition has it that Drake commented, 'There is time to finish the game and beat the Spaniards too.' Drake knew that the tide had at least three hours to run before his fleet could begin to move out of port.

By noon the following day, most of the fifty-four English ships were at sea. This had been skilfully achieved against the wind. A further ten joined them, making a total force from Plymouth of sixty-four, twenty-four of them fighting vessels.

A west-south-westerly was blowing the Spanish Armada slowly up the Channel. It was an awe-inspiring sight – a neat formation of 130 ships in the form of a crescent. At the centre was the main battle-fleet under Medina Sidonia and at the crescent tips were his best fighting ships, including galleasses – full three-masted galleons with a company of rowers. It was a

Portrait of Queen Elizabeth I attributed to Frederico Zucchero, which now hangs in Buckland Abbey

brilliant show of military precision – for as long as the wind was favourable.

The English fleet, with Howard on his flagship, the *Ark Royal,* and Drake in command of the *Revenge,* moved to the south and north points of the crescent and fired on the Armada. It was an inconclusive action, but Medina Sidonia and his officers were

Map of the English Channel, showing the ships of the Armada in crescent formation and the English fleet emerging from Plymouth

alarmed at the small size and agility of the English ships and, from this moment, began doubting their chances of success. They were only there at Philip's insistence, for he had written, 'No step must . . . be taken by us to interrupt the course of the Divine purpose.' Although Howard and Drake believed that the Spanish intended to land at several points along the coast, Medina Sidonia was only planning to sail to the Low Countries, where the main land army was to be collected.

News of the Armada's arrival soon spread. Beacons had been lit at the very first sightings and small armies of territorials stood by along the whole of the south coast. Everything was prepared to fight off an invasion. Drake, in the *Revenge,* stayed close to the Spanish fleet, intent on preventing a landing, with Howard following in the *Ark Royal.*

On the afternoon of 21 July, a massive explosion of gun-powder on the *San Salvador* forced the Spanish fleet to drop sail and help to pick up casualties. In the ensuing chaos, the *Nuestra Señora del Rosario* rammed the *Santa Catalina,* and, unable to make sail, she fell back, isolated from the main ships. By a strange and lucky chance, Drake had broken away from the English fleet to attack a group of ships which turned out to be innocent German traders, and stumbled on the floundering *Rosario.* On board, he discovered chests of treasure and a large quantity of coins. The vessel was impounded at Torbay and her captain, Pedro de Valdes, was to be Drake's prisoner until, three years later, his family in Spain was able to raise three thousand pounds to have him released.

By 24 July, after two days of skirmishing and harassment, the two fleets were off the Isle of Wight. Drake and the English captains knew these waters well and attempted to drive the Armada on to the Owers, a treacherous area of rocks and shoal. The Spanish ships sighted the hazard just in time, and tacked away to the south-east and then towards Calais. They were seriously short of ammunition and provisions. An urgent message was sent, advising the Duke of Parma of the fleet's intention to meet the land army at Dunkirk.

In the Spanish Netherlands, Parma had been making strenuous efforts during the previous year to prepare his army for the invasion of England. Canals had been cut and channels deepened to allow the 166 barges which were to carry the troops a clear passage from the shallow estuaries into the English Channel. But Parma's preparations had been hampered by the presence of Dutch Protestant rebels, who controlled the coastal waters. If the barges were to move out into deeper water, they would be exposed to attack.

As Medina Sidonia dropped anchor off Calais on 27 July, he received grim news. The Spanish forces, due to embark at Dunkirk and Flushing, were not ready. It is now thought that Parma, not believing in the feasibility of such a grand venture, had withdrawn from the invasion entirely. As Medina Sidonia received the news, the entire English fleet of 140 vessels, including Seymour's ships from Dover, was seen bearing down on the Armada.

At midnight, as the tide ran to advantage, Howard sent eight fireships into the midst of the Spanish fleet. They were manned by crews ready to jump into longboats towed at their sides. A Spanish officer later wrote, 'Every vessel was forced to shift itself thence as best it could, flying from so great a peril as that which stared us in the face.' Fearing explosion, the Armada was thrown into chaos, driven out to sea, and dispersed. The commander,

The route of the Armada through the English Channel

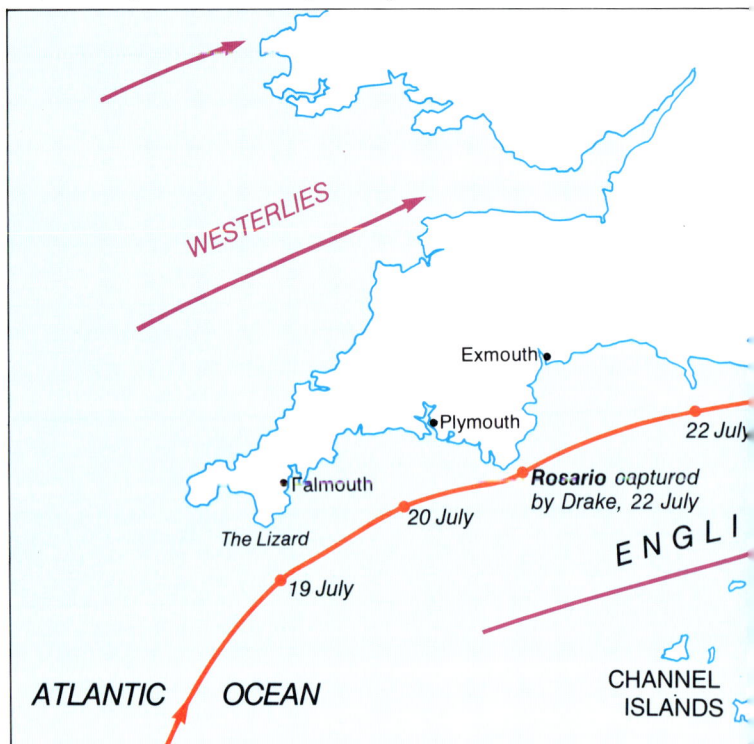

Medina Sidonia, in his flagship, the *San Martin,* managed to rally a few of his ships. At this moment, Drake, on the *Revenge,* moved in alongside and, as the two ships passed within a hundred yards, both came under intense fire. The *San Martin* survived the attack, mainly due to its sturdy construction. Heavy casualties were suffered on both sides. The Spanish fleet was scattered, but by brilliant and courageous seamanship was able to reform into a crescent of about fifty ships to the north of Calais at Gravelines and, for the whole of the day of 29 July, was fired

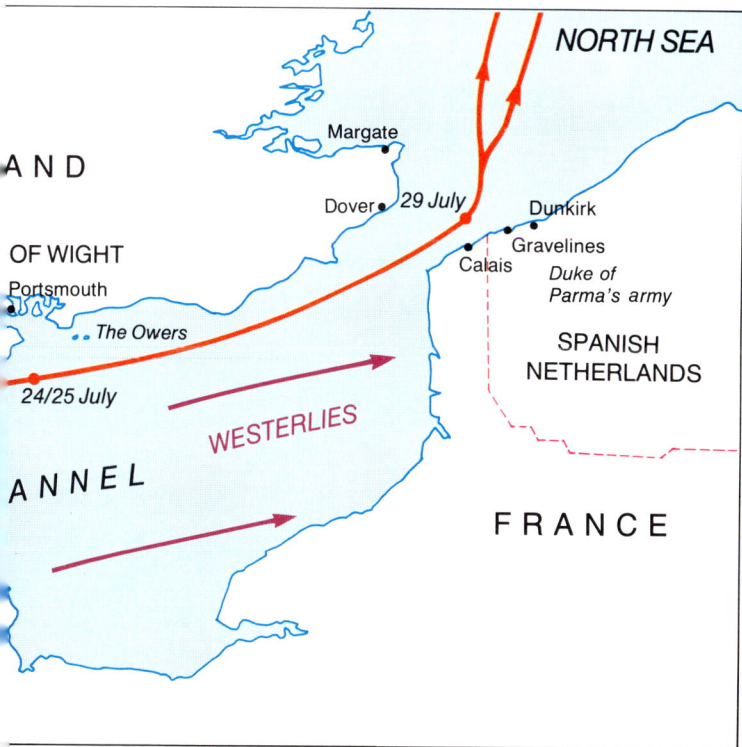

Overleaf: *Fireships burning at Calais*

upon by the English. In the early evening, a squall hit both fleets and, when it cleared, the Spanish ships were seen moving north in tight formation.

Medina Sidonia's sailing orders were to return home by whatever means possible and it was now clear that the only route back to Spain was round the coast of Scotland. The English fleet was not to know this, and followed the stricken Spanish ships, all the time fearing a possible landing by Medina Sidonia on the east coast of England. The Duke of Parma would then have been able to move his forces across the unguarded Channel. However Medina Sidonia was only concerned to return to Spain. Drake and Howard chased his fleet as far as the Firth of Forth, where, running out of food, water and ammunition, they turned back.

The Armada was defeated and Drake was to write later, 'There was never anything please me better than seeing the enemy flying with a southerly wind to the northwards.'

Escape around Scotland

The Spanish ships struggled northwards, sometimes in groups, sometimes singly. To save drinking water, Medina Sidonia ordered that all horses and mules should be driven overboard. A Danish merchant-ship later reported sailing through a mass of swimming animals with no ships in sight to explain the phenomenon. Two ships were lost as the fleet passed round the treacherous north coast of Scotland. As they sailed westward to Ireland, many Spaniards died of hunger or thirst. Some vessels just sank; more than twenty-four ships were wrecked on the Irish coast. The men who managed to swim to land were stripped of their possessions by the local people. Most were then killed by the English garrisons stationed in Ireland.

Recent underwater salvage has uncovered fascinating relics from some of these Spanish galleons. On the galleass *Girona,* lost close by the Giant's Causeway, County Antrim, have been found precious jewels, and coins minted from the gold and silver of Mexico and Peru. The entire collection, saved from dispersal, is now in the Ulster Museum, Belfast.

At the end of September 1588, the remains of the fleet began arriving back at the Spanish port of Santander. The flagship, the *San Martin,* carried 200 bodies, and the remainder of the crew was ill and starving. Of the 130 ships that had sailed on the 'Enterprise of England', over sixty had been lost.

In England it was gradually realised that a great victory had been achieved. Protestant England had been delivered from the might of Catholic Spain.

A gold salamander pendant set with rubies and five of the 1,200 gold and silver escudo pieces recovered from the wreck of the Girona. *Overleaf: The route taken by the Armada*

SKOTLANDE

NORWAYE

DEN MARKE

FRISLANDE

HOLLAND

BRABANTE

FLANDERS

PICARDIE

ENGLANDE

YORKE

BRISTOL

LONDON

NORMANDIE

EAST

Out of favour

English naval power had been proved superior to that of Spain and Drake gloried in the success the fleet had achieved. Early the following year news came that Philip, angered by defeat, was preparing a new Armada. Drake, financed by an enthusiastic syndicate with Elizabeth as the chief shareholder, set sail for Spain and Portugal, carrying over 10,000 soldiers. The aim was to attack ports, including Lisbon, and to disrupt and plunder. The Queen hoped that the forces would destroy what was left of the Spanish navy and then place the Portuguese prince, Don Antonio, on the throne of Portugal. Don Antonio promised to grant full rights for England to trade with the East Indies.

Although this was the largest fleet ever to set sail from England, the campaign was not a triumph. Once the soldiers had been landed, communication between Drake and Sir John Norris, who was in charge of the land force, broke down. An assault on Corunna was only partly successful, despite Norris's achievement in heading off a Spanish force which intended to relieve the city. The difficulties of coordinating a land and sea attack on Lisbon, by now fully prepared, proved overwhelming. The city did not rise in support of Don Antonio as hoped.

Drake and his fleet eventually turned for home. There had been some success in disrupting life on the Spanish and Portuguese coastline, and coastal trade had been interrupted. A group of Hanseatic corn hulks had been intercepted and sunk. But although weakening Spanish sea power, the venture did not, as intended, finally end Spanish domination of the oceans.

Drake was now out of favour with the Queen. After the extraordinary success against the Armada, the recent campaign seemed a failure. The investors, including Elizabeth, had lost a large amount of money, and the aims of destroying the Spanish navy and putting a friendly prince on the throne of Portugal had not been achieved. Norris and the land army took what credit there was for success at Corunna and the power of the English navy seemed to have diminished. For Drake, this signalled the end of a great career.

Final years

Drake returned to Devon, where he enjoyed the country pursuits of Buckland – hunting stag, fishing in the Tavy and arranging concerts of his favourite music. He busied himself in his home town of Plymouth, planning new defences. In 1590 he was appointed to bring fresh water to the town, having experienced many years of problems with carting fresh water to ships in Plymouth harbour. A seventeen-mile open channel was cut to divert water from the River Meavy on Dartmoor to provide a supply for the town. Drake's Leat, as it became known, was to be Plymouth's main source of water for 300 years.

Drake's Leat, on Dartmoor, which supplied water to Plymouth from the River Meavy for 300 years

On the day of its opening, 23 April 1591, the Mayor and Corporation rode out of the town along the dry bed of the leat, followed by the excited people of Plymouth. Drake meanwhile had ridden ahead to the top of the channel, on Dartmoor, and took pleasure in riding beside the flow of water as it was released down the leat, much to the delight of the crowds.

In 1591 news came of the death of Sir Richard Grenville, former owner of Buckland Abbey, who had been killed at sea on Drake's old flagship, the *Revenge.*

As Member of Parliament for Bossinney, Drake frequently visited London. At Court, in Parliament and in the City, with his West Country friends, he took on an energetic role in planning and administrating matters to do with the sea.

Drake's last voyage

In 1595 Parliament was persuaded to finance a major expedition to the West Indies, led by Drake and Sir John Hawkyns. It was intended, once again, to weaken the power of Spain and capture more treasure. Drake hoped that this voyage would rekindle in him his youthful energies. He was now in his early fifties, a good age in those days, with a greying beard and wide stocky frame.

No sooner had the fleet dropped anchor off San Juan in Puerto Rico, than news came of Hawkyns' death aboard the *Garland* from a fever. His last words were '. . . that he saw no other but danger of ruin likely to ensue of the whole voyage'.

In spite of this sad event, Drake continued with his plans to capture the treasure-store, but the town was now well fortified and he was forced to retreat out to sea with heavy casualties. Drake turned the fleet towards Panama, attacking the almost deserted town of Rio de la Hacha and passing Cartagena. At Nombre de Dios he looted the town, but found no treasure.

Drake planned a land attack on the Isthmus of Panama, but the situation had changed in the ten years since he was last in the Caribbean. A raiding party, under the senior military officer, Sir

Drake's Drum, carried on the Defiance *on Drake's last voyage and brought back by his crew to rest in a place of honour in Buckland Abbey*

Thomas Baskerville, found no trace of the mule-trains. The men were ambushed and finally arrived back on the coast with little to show for their efforts.

It was clear that there remained nothing to gain from this enterprise. Ironically, Drake was now suffering the effects of his previous achievements. The continual harassment of the Spanish colonies over many years had been successful. Many of

The Burial of Admiral Drake, *by Thomas Davidson, which can be seen in Buckland Abbey*

the settlements were empty and shipping had diminished. The kingdom of Spain no longer dominated the Caribbean.

Dysentery was spreading through all the crews, and on 23 January 1596 Drake himself fell ill and had to remain in his cabin on the *Defiance*. Even so, he retained command and ordered that the fleet should sail to Puerto Bello. On 27 January, Drake realised that the end was near and summoned the energy to make a will, bequeathing his property to his younger brother, Thomas. Elizabeth Drake already had a life interest in Buckland Abbey. During the night, Drake became delirious and insisted on donning his armour '. . . to die like a soldier'. At four the next morning he died. Drake was about fifty-five years of age. The next day, he was buried at sea in a lead coffin to the sound of trumpets, drums and cannons. A brilliant and courageous life had ended.